She
Persisted

DOLORES HUERTA

— INSPIRED BY —
She Persisted
by Chelsea Clinton & Alexandra Boiger

DOLORES HUERTA

Written by
Monica Brown

Interior illustrations by
Gillian Flint

PHILOMEL

PHILOMEL
An imprint of Penguin Random House LLC
1745 Broadway, New York, New York 10019

First published in the United States of America by Philomel,
an imprint of Penguin Random House LLC, 2024

Text copyright © 2024 by Chelsea Clinton
Illustrations copyright © 2024 by Alexandra Boiger

Penguin supports copyright. Copyright fuels creativity, encourages diverse voices, promotes free speech, and creates a vibrant culture. Thank you for buying an authorized edition of this book and for complying with copyright laws by not reproducing, scanning, or distributing any part of it in any form without permission. You are supporting writers and allowing Penguin to continue to publish books for every reader.

Philomel is a registered trademark of Penguin Random House LLC.
The Penguin colophon is a registered trademark of Penguin Books Limited.

Visit us online at PenguinRandomHouse.com.

Library of Congress Cataloging-in-Publication Data is available.

ISBN 9780593623565 (hardcover)
ISBN 9780593623572 (paperback)

1st Printing

Printed in the United States of America

LSCC

Edited by Talia Benamy.
Design by Ellice M. Lee.
Text set in LTC Kennerley Pro.

The publisher does not have any control over and does not assume any responsibility for author or third-party websites or their content.

⧼ To ⧽
Dolores Huerta and all who advocate
for justice and peace

Dear Reader,

As Sally Ride and Marian Wright Edelman both powerfully said, "You can't be what you can't see." When Sally said that, she meant that it was hard to dream of being an astronaut, like she was, or a doctor or an athlete or anything at all if you didn't see someone like you who already had lived that dream. She especially was talking about seeing women in jobs that historically were held by men.

I wrote the first *She Persisted* and the books that came after it because I wanted young girls—and children of all genders—to see women who worked hard to live their dreams. And I wanted all of us to see examples of persistence in the face of different challenges to help inspire us in our own lives.

I'm so thrilled now to partner with a sisterhood of writers to bring longer, more in-depth versions of these stories of women's persistence and achievement to readers. I hope you enjoy these chapter books as much as I do and find them inspiring and empowering.

And remember: If anyone ever tells you no, if anyone ever says your voice isn't important or your dreams are too big, remember these women. They persisted and so should you.

Warmly,

Chelsea Clinton

She Persisted

She Persisted: MARIAN ANDERSON

She Persisted: VIRGINIA APGAR

She Persisted: PURA BELPRÉ

She Persisted: SIMONE BILES

She Persisted: NELLIE BLY

She Persisted: RUBY BRIDGES

She Persisted: KALPANA CHAWLA

She Persisted: CLAUDETTE COLVIN

She Persisted: ELLA FITZGERALD

She Persisted: ROSALIND FRANKLIN

She Persisted: TEMPLE GRANDIN

She Persisted: DEB HAALAND

She Persisted: BETHANY HAMILTON

She Persisted: DOROTHY HEIGHT

She Persisted: DOLORES HUERTA

She Persisted: FLORENCE GRIFFITH JOYNER

She Persisted: HELEN KELLER

She Persisted: CORETTA SCOTT KING

She Persisted: OPAL LEE

She Persisted: CLARA LEMLICH

She Persisted: RACHEL LEVINE

She Persisted: MAYA LIN

She Persisted: WANGARI MAATHAI

She Persisted: WILMA MANKILLER

She Persisted: PATSY MINK

She Persisted: FLORENCE NIGHTINGALE

She Persisted: NAOMI OSAKA

She Persisted: SALLY RIDE

She Persisted: MARGARET CHASE SMITH

She Persisted: SONIA SOTOMAYOR

She Persisted: MARIA TALLCHIEF

She Persisted: DIANA TAURASI

She Persisted: HARRIET TUBMAN

She Persisted: OPRAH WINFREY

She Persisted: MALALA YOUSAFZAI

DOLORES HUERTA

TABLE OF CONTENTS

....

Chapter 1: *Early Years* 1

Chapter 2: *Serving Others* 9

Chapter 3: *Sharing in the Harvest* 19

Chapter 4: *¡Sí, Se Puede! Yes, You Can!* 29

Chapter 5: *And Justice for All* 38

Chapter 6: *Legacy* 46

How You Can Persist 54

References 60

CHAPTER 1

Early Years

On April 10, 1930, in the small mining town of Dawson, New Mexico, a great leader was born. When Juan Fernández and Alicia Chávez first held their daughter, Dolores Clara Fernández, in their arms, they didn't know that she would grow up to be Dolores Huerta, a powerful labor leader and activist inspiring thousands in the fight for justice.

Dolores's father, Juan, the child of Mexican

immigrants, worked in the coal mines—a very dangerous job. Over the years, hundreds of workers, mostly immigrants from Mexico, Greece, and Italy, lost their lives in explosions and unsafe working conditions. Money was still tight, so to earn a bit more, her father also worked in the fields, and conditions as a farmworker were also very hard.

Dolores's parents divorced when she was a toddler, and she was only six when her mother moved the family to Stockton, California. Dolores didn't see her father often growing up, but she knew he was a union organizer. A union organizer is someone who helps workers form a labor union so that they can act collectively—as a unit—to gain better working conditions. He also believed in political participation and ran for political office. When he was elected to the New Mexico

State Legislature, Dolores was very proud.

It was Dolores's mother, Alicia, however, who was Dolores's greatest inspiration. As a single mother in Stockton, Alicia worked two jobs to support Dolores and her two brothers— as a waitress during the day and as a cannery worker at night. They lived in a diverse community that included Mexican, Black, Chinese, Filipino, and Japanese farmworkers. Alicia was an active community and church member, and she taught Dolores the value of hard work, independence, and community involvement. When she eventually ended up owning and running a hotel, Dolores's mother would offer discounts to poor migrant families, and if they were in crisis, she wouldn't charge them at all.

Dolores's mother taught her to help people

in need *before* they asked, and to never try to get credit for it. From her mother, Dolores learned compassion, and that taking care of others was more important than making money.

Young Dolores was bright and curious and filled with energy. She loved to dance! Dolores and her brothers were often cared for by their grandfather Herculano Chávez, who would joke that Dolores must have seven tongues because she talked so much. Dolores's fast tongue would one day serve her well when she gave speeches and made arguments in front of politicians and legislators.

Even though she was the only girl in the family, Dolores was not made to serve her two brothers or do more house chores than them, which was common practice in other families. In

Dolores's house, everyone was treated equally. Unfortunately, this wasn't the case outside her home and in her high school.

Dolores learned early on about discrimination. In high school, Dolores studied hard, staying up late to work on her papers. She was a great writer and got straight As, but at the end of the year the teacher gave her a lower grade and accused her of cheating. The teacher didn't believe a Mexican American student could have written such excellent papers. This did not stop Dolores from pursuing her education, though. If someone told Dolores that she couldn't do something, she decided that yes, she could!

Her mother encouraged Dolores to become active in the community. Dolores joined the Girl Scouts and held fundraisers to support soldiers in

··· 6 ···

World War II. In high school, she participated in different community youth organizations. Some held dances to raise money for baskets for the poor. But as she got older, Dolores realized that she wanted to do more. She thought it would be more powerful if the working poor could advocate for themselves and their communities, fighting together for lasting change.

CHAPTER 2

Serving Others

After high school, Dolores went to Stockton College, where she was often the only Mexican American in her classes. While in college, she married her high school boyfriend, Ralph Head, and had two daughters, Celeste and Lori. Dolores earned a teaching certificate and began teaching the children of local farmworkers in Stockton. She saw them come to school in bare feet and too hungry to learn as best as they

could. Dolores believed that no child should go to school hungry, but she also realized that donating food was a short-term solution. She instead asked herself: Why are working families unable to feed their kids? It was clear that the large farming corporations, called agribusinesses, were taking advantage of their workers. Why couldn't the farmworkers who grew the food that wound up on so many people's tables share in the harvest?

In the mid-1950s, Dolores met the community organizer Fred Ross, who changed the path of her life forever. Fred Ross had co-founded the Community Service Organization (CSO) a few years earlier with Latino leaders Edward Roybal and Antonio Ríos. The CSO was a successful Mexican American civil rights organization that fought discrimination and organized Mexican communities to act together for change. Dolores wanted to change the circumstances that created poverty in their community and was inspired by Fred to use the power of organizing to improve lives. She joined the CSO in 1955.

Fred Ross saw great potential in Dolores. She was a natural leader—smart, bold, courageous, and deeply committed to social justice. In the CSO, Dolores worked to register voters, teach citizenship classes, and improve living conditions in the barrios, where many Mexican Americans lived. If the Mexican American communities were more organized as voters, they would have more political power and be more successful in making changes. With Fred's mentorship, Dolores was instrumental in growing the Stockton chapter.

This was also a time of personal change

for Dolores. She divorced her first husband and married Ventura Huerta, who also worked for the CSO. Together, they had five children—Fidel, Emilio, Vincent, Alicia, and Angela. Despite being an organizer himself, Dolores's husband resented the time she spent away from the home, childcare, and housework. These expectations were common for women of that time period. But Dolores Huerta's mother had taught her to believe that men and women were equal, so despite her husband's criticism, she decided to pursue her path of leadership. Dolores felt passionate in her calling to serve not only her own family, but her entire community. She wanted to make a broad impact, which is exactly what she did.

Dolores was soon given greater responsibilities and became a lobbyist for the CSO, working directly with legislators to advocate for change. She was the first Mexican American lobbyist in Sacramento, and state senators grew to fear and respect her, even if they didn't agree with her.

At the state capitol, Dolores had many successes! She helped secure disability insurance for farmworkers and retirement plans for the noncitizens who worked in the United States, a long-lasting achievement that still impacts lives today.

But Dolores didn't stop there. In 1958, she and other CSO colleagues founded the Agricultural Workers Association. The problems facing farmworkers were unique. They were exposed to poisonous pesticides (many of which are no longer allowed to be used today) and worked in the hot sun without access to restrooms, soap, or fresh water. Often, they made less than a dollar an hour for demanding, backbreaking work. It was no wonder they struggled to feed their families.

Dolores Huerta was not the only leader who Fred Ross mentored. Years earlier, he had met a young man named César Chávez, in whom he saw incredible talent and promise. César had a deep commitment to social justice and a rare ability to inspire others. César rose quickly in the CSO and was the executive director when he and Dolores Huerta finally met and began working together. They recognized each other's talents. César Chávez admired Dolores's courage, intelligence, and dedication. Dolores admired César's vision, spirituality, and commitment to the working poor.

Most important, they both wanted to improve the lives of farmworkers. César and his wife, Helen, had both worked in the fields, just as Dolores's father had. Their personal and family experiences influenced their work. The corporate growers were powerful and more interested in profit than people. For example, when the growers needed to spray plants with pesticides, they would do so from above—which meant that the spray would also land on the workers, making them ill. Farmworkers were in the fields from sunup to sundown and had little stability. They had to move with the crops, which was hard on their children.

Together, Dolores and César asked, where was the justice?

CHAPTER 3

Sharing in the Harvest

César and Dolores shared a dream: organizing a farmworkers union. If workers could bargain and negotiate with employers collectively, they would have more power. The labor movement in the United States had picked up steam in the late 1800s, as workers learned to organize, form unions, and come together to pressure employers for living wages, benefits, safer working conditions, and time to rest. But

farmworkers had never been organized into a union.

César and Dolores worked within the Community Service Organization to support farmworkers, but they felt the CSO wasn't doing enough. One day, César invited Dolores to his home to talk about a farmworkers union. "If you and I don't do it, it's never going to happen," he said. They worried that the growers were too powerful and too racist, but in the name of justice, they had to try.

On March 31, 1962, César's birthday, he resigned from the CSO and moved to Delano, California, in the Central Valley, where so many families—mothers, fathers, and children—bent over the fields of rich farmland, picking fruits and vegetables in terrible working conditions and scorching heat. Together with Dolores, César founded the National Farm Workers Association (NFWA). Even as César became the most public face of the union, they were a team. He explained that "Dolores and I were the architects of the National Farm Workers Association."

At first, Dolores kept working for the CSO while also doing farmworker organizing. But before long, she realized that she couldn't keep doing both. Dolores was in the middle of a divorce from her second husband and had seven children to feed. César said, "You can't work for a living and fight. You've got to do one or the other." She wondered, could she leave stability behind to move to Delano and devote her life full-time to organizing farmworkers with César? Yes, she could. To make it work, she had to leave some of her children with relatives, and she was so poor, she moved in with César; his wife, Helen; and their eight children for a time. But it was worth it for the work she felt called to do.

Together, Dolores and César grew the organization by holding house meetings in workers' homes to recruit them to la causa, the cause. They explained that the workers could be stronger together and asked for their help spreading the message. Soon this led to larger general meetings, and then, in 1963, they had the first NFWA constitutional convention in Fresno, California. César was named president, and Dolores was named vice president alongside Julio Hernández and Gilbert Padilla.

Dolores traveled constantly for the union and was away from her children, which was

difficult for her—and them. Still, she persisted. She was barely surviving financially, as union workers made only five dollars a week. When she had to, she would work as a substitute teacher to help pay bills. Her children did not grow up with privilege, but Dolores decided that if she couldn't give her children material things, she would give them something more important: a social consciousness and a good set of values. Though Dolores brought her children with her as often as she could, her oldest daughters helped raise the younger children, as did various family and community members. As her son Emilio once said, "My mother really didn't belong to us." She belonged to the movement. And no one in the movement would starve, because they took care of each other.

Dolores and César drew from existing organizing strategies and also created their own. The NFWA had different tools: They could strike and refuse to do their jobs to pressure employers to make concessions, but sometimes growers just brought in strikebreakers—other workers. The union could also organize a boycott, which meant asking the public to support their protest by refusing to buy certain vegetables or fruits until growers offered better working conditions. Consumer boycotts impacted agribusinesses in the area they cared about most—making money. Workers could march too, though sometimes the growers would threaten marchers or bribe the police to violently break them up.

The union also lobbied politicians at state capitols, working directly with legislators, Dolores's strength. The NFWA would go on to use each one of these organizing tools successfully! But the most important principle underlying any action the union took was that of nonviolence. Inspired by leaders such as Mahatma Gandhi and the Reverend Martin Luther King Jr., the union committed to achieving their goals without the use of any force, because justice was on their side.

This would become very important during the union's very first strike.

CHAPTER 4

. . . .

¡Sí, Se Puede! Yes, You Can!

In 1965, when Dolores and César were early in the process of building up membership in the union among Mexican farmworkers, they were approached by a group of Filipino farmworkers who had decided to strike against table-grape growers. Though the union was young, they voted to join the strike a week later, in solidarity for all workers!

In support of the strike, Dolores Huerta led the national grape boycott, bringing it to the attention of millions of American consumers. In 1966, César led a 340-mile march from Delano to the steps of the state capitol in Sacramento to gain national attention for the strike. The big corporations sometimes used violence and intimidation with the striking workers. When César felt that members were getting frustrated and wanting to fight back, he went on a hunger strike, or fast, to help people remember their commitment to nonviolence. César believed that protests should be peaceful and grounded in love.

As the strike went on for several years, Dolores and César gained national attention for the cause. One of their biggest supporters was Attorney General Robert "Bobby" Kennedy, who ran for president in 1968. The NFWA was involved in local and national politics, running voter registration and education drives. They supported Bobby Kennedy and helped him win the Democratic primary in California. Dolores stood by Bobby's side as he gave his victory speech and thanked his friend Dolores and the farmworkers for their support. The celebratory night would turn tragic, however, when Bobby Kennedy was assassinated minutes later. Dolores was devastated but didn't let the death of her friend and supporter stop her efforts, because she knew Bobby would have wanted her to keep on working for justice and nonviolence.

It was a multiyear process, but even though agribusiness had the laws and money on their side, the National Farm Workers Association was ultimately successful. In 1970, when the association signed a historic agreement with twenty-six

$\cdots$ 31 $\cdots$

table-grape growers, Dolores Huerta negotiated the contract! It was a great victory for the union and the community.

Of course, Dolores knew there was more work to do, and more workers to empower.

The National Farm Workers Association was renamed the United Farm Workers (UFW) in 1972, the same year César began a twenty-five-day fast in Arizona to draw attention to the plight of farmworkers there. The workers were afraid to risk fighting the growers for better working conditions, and Dolores and César met resistance. "We can't do it," they told Dolores at a meeting, "we can't do it." Dolores believed it *could* be done, so she replied, "¡Sí, se puede! Yes, you can!" This would soon become a rallying cry for the union and for organizers everywhere. One day many

years later, future president Barack Obama would borrow the phrase "Yes, we can!" during his successful campaign for president of the United States in 2008.

César and Dolores had a great partnership, though they often argued. Dolores was nicknamed "la Pasionaria," the passionate one. But despite their different styles, César valued Dolores's honesty and insight, as she valued his. Using their complementary talents and skills, Dolores and César had many great victories! In 1975, the California Agricultural Labor Relations Act was passed, recognizing the right of farmworkers there to bargain collectively. The UFW also led efforts in 1986 to pass the federal Immigration Reform and Control Act, which offered amnesty to millions of undocumented migrants who had come into the United States before 1982. Farmworkers who could show that they had jobs for at least three months were allowed to live legally in the United States. César and Dolores's work together in California was influencing laws throughout the entire country and creating better conditions for farmworkers and their families.

During this period of union growth and activism, Dolores entered into a loving relationship with the person who would become her life partner, union activist Richard Chávez, César's brother. Richard, in fact, was the designer of the famous UFW flag with its bold eagle. Side by side, they too worked for justice, and together they welcomed four children, Juana, Maria Elena, Ricardo, and Camila. They were together until Richard's death in 2011.

CHAPTER 5

And Justice for All

Dolores continued to work tirelessly for the union, supporting boycotts and legislative efforts and speaking to the press, noting that "none of us can live without food, none of us can live without what is produced in our fields . . . this is life, and yet, these are the worst paid workers on the planet." She never missed an opportunity to inspire others to believe that everyone should share in the harvest!

Her pursuit of justice expanded to include the rights of others, not only farmworkers. While working for the union, Dolores Huerta grew as a leader—and as a feminist, advocating for equal rights for women. She was responsible for bringing many women *into* the labor movement. Although women had positions of great importance in the union, leading clinics and as field directors, the executive board members were all men in the early years—except for Dolores. And when history was written, the women were left out.

As a board member, Dolores challenged discrimination against women in the union and slowly educated her male colleagues about it. At one board meeting, she took note of each negative remark made about women and their abilities.

At the end of the meeting, when César asked if anyone had anything to add, Dolores said, "Yes, I just want to mention that during the course of this meeting all of you have made fifty-eight chauvinist remarks against women." Dolores did that in every meeting until the men eventually stopped making such comments. She was at the forefront of creating a more inclusive union.

Dolores was inspired by her own mother's vision of equality, and she was also inspired by others working for the rights of women. During the grape boycott she was directing in the late 1960s from New York City, Dolores met Gloria Steinem and other leaders of the growing women's rights movement. Dolores became involved in the Feminist Majority Foundation (FMF), a nonprofit group dedicated to women's equality in politics and everywhere. She was a passionate supporter of women candidates and would one day campaign for the first female Democratic nominee for president, former Secretary of State Hillary Rodham Clinton.

Dolores's work for the union was often dangerous. Over the course of her life as an activist, she was arrested more than twenty times. She didn't feel sorry for herself, though. Dolores believed that experiencing the humiliation of losing her bodily freedom gave her more compassion for those wrongly imprisoned. In 1988, while protesting the political policies of future president George H. W. Bush, Dolores, who was only five feet and two inches tall and weighed just 110 pounds, was severely beaten by a police officer in San Francisco. She was hospitalized with broken ribs and a shattered spleen. César visited her in the hospital.

After that, Dolores, the tireless fighter, was forced to take a break to heal. It was difficult for the woman who wanted to take care of others to

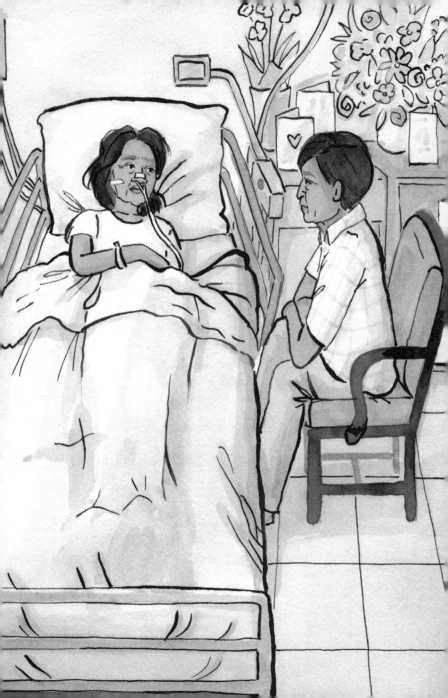

rest and be taken care of, but her children and community surrounded her with love. And still she fought. As a public figure, Dolores could bring attention to the excessive use of force, so she sued the city of San Francisco and won a settlement and a commitment for better training for police officers. After she healed, she took a leave from the union to work with the FMF and focus on electing more Latinas to political office.

On April 23, 1993, César, Dolores's friend and co-leader of three decades, died. Dolores was devastated, as were many across the country and world. She came together with thousands to march and mourn the man who had believed that empowered people change history. It was difficult to go on, but Dolores continued to work for the farmworkers. In 1999, at age sixty-nine, Dolores made the difficult decision to step away from leadership in the union to pursue new pathways toward justice.

Dolores never stopped marching and advocating for farmworkers—she just spread her arms even wider. As Dolores worked on behalf of women, immigrants, and the working poor, she inspired a new generation of leaders. When President Bill Clinton chose Dolores as one of five recipients of the Eleanor Roosevelt Award for Human Rights, he thanked her for "all you have done and all you still do to promote the dignity and human rights of America's family."

CHAPTER 6

Legacy

Dolores Huerta continued to sow the seeds of justice into her eighties and nineties. When she faced challenges, Dolores liked to quote the poet Pablo Neruda, who said, "They can cut all the flowers, but they can't hold back the spring." In 2002, Dolores Huerta received the Puffin Prize for Creative Citizenship, which honors an "individual who has challenged the status quo through distinctive, courageous, imaginative and socially responsible work of significance." The award came with a $100,000 prize. How would Dolores use the money? Would she spend it on herself? Of course not!

Dolores wanted to continue to serve her community and mentor the next generation of activists, so in 2003 she started the Dolores Huerta Foundation. A foundation is a nonprofit or charitable trust that can sponsor other organizations or institutions that support similar goals. The Dolores Huerta Foundation's central mission is "inspiring and organizing communities to build volunteer organizations empowered to pursue social justice."

The Dolores Huerta Foundation shares the message of people power. Dolores continues to believe that when people work together with others, they can use their voices and power to make change in their communities. Her foundation supports educational and health equity, LGBTQ+ rights, workers' rights, and immigrant rights.

One of the foundation's early initiatives brought Dolores back to her beginnings of organizing house meetings for the young union. The foundation's Vecinos Unidos (Neighbors United) program offered leadership training to neighborhood groups, who then worked to hold elected officials accountable and make sure they do what they promised. It has encouraged neighborhood folks to have a voice in local politics, and together they have successfully advocated for more parks, paved roads, and better sewage connections in the Central Valley in California. The foundation fought (and continues to fight) against discrimination and inequity, and during times of crisis, it offers aid. Dolores also has a particular passion for training the next generation of leaders through Dolores Huerta Foundation youth programs such as Liberated Youth for Empowerment (LYFE).

In 2011, President Barack Obama honored Dolores with the Presidential Medal of Freedom. This is the United States' highest civilian award, and it recognizes "an especially meritorious contribution to the security or national interests of the United States, world peace, cultural or other significant public or private endeavors." When Dolores accepted the award, she said, "The freedom of association means that people can come together in organization to fight for solutions to the problems they confront in their communities.

The great social justice changes in our country have happened when people came together, organized, and took direct action. It is this right that sustains and nurtures our democracy today. The civil rights movement, the labor movement, the women's movement, and the equality movement for our LGBT brothers and sisters are all manifestations of these rights."

Dolores Huerta wants young people to know that voting is as important as marching. After being named *Glamour* magazine's woman of the year, she explained: ". . . if we do not put some of these things that we want, progressive changes, into a law, it's not going to make any difference . . . Yes, take that march. But you got to march right to the ballot box." She also wants to make sure that women are not left out of the history of the movement, given that they've been at the front lines all along.

Today, in her nineties, Dolores Huerta persists in her fight for social justice and equality for all. She continues to inspire others to join her in the march for justice. She continues to speak out, organize, and march because there is so much more to be done. The Dolores Huerta Foundation is now working to establish the Dolores Huerta Peace and Justice Cultural Center in downtown Bakersfield, California, Dolores's home city. And Dolores continues to believe that "every moment is an organizing opportunity, every person a potential activist, every minute a chance to change the world." And we believe her, because for well over sixty years, that is exactly what Dolores did. And continues to do.

So when you feel like giving up or think that you just can't do something, just remember what Dolores taught us all: "¡Sí, se puede! Yes, you can!"

HOW YOU CAN PERSIST

by Monica Brown

If you admire Dolores Huerta's community activism and social justice work and want to contribute to her legacy, here are some activities for you to explore.

1. Learn more about the hands that bring food to your table. Go to your school or public library and research the lives of farmworkers in the United States.

Who else works to supply the food we eat? Learn more about factory workers, truck drivers, grocery store workers, and everyone who brings the harvest to you!

2. Women made a great impact in the labor movement. Dolores Huerta is one in a long line of leaders. Learn about other woman labor leaders such as Dorothy Day, Velma Hopkins, Mother Jones, Clara Lemlich, Luisa Moreno, Francis Perkins, and Emma Tenayuca.

3. Dolores Huerta is a community organizer. Who is part of your community? And how might you make your community better? With a caregiver's or teacher's permission

and supervision, think about ways you can support and improve the lives of the people around you. This might look like helping an elderly neighbor, volunteering at your local food bank, organizing a community cleanup or recycling effort, or supporting the workers in your community in some small or large way.

4. Is there an issue, problem, or challenge you feel passionately about? Talk with your parents and teachers. Identify the problem and potential solutions. Start a petition. Write a letter. You can even organize a letter-writing campaign by asking others to also write letters to those who might be able to help solve

the issue you're facing! This might mean writing letters to your teachers, your school administrators, political officials, or the local newspaper!

5. Dolores Huerta was very involved in voter registration and education. Why do you think voting is important? Create a mock election at your school—or in your family! Name an issue, create voter registration forms that must be filled out by a specific date, and set up a ballot box. Perhaps set up a debate about the issue. Encourage the adults in your life to vote in local, state, and national elections, and get ready for the future when you can vote on your own!

6. Learn more about Labor Day, the national holiday that honors workers and their achievements! It was nineteenth-century labor activists who first advocated for this work holiday that takes place each year on the first Monday in September. Read more about it here: dol.gov/general/laborday /history.

7. When someone tells you that you can't get something done or that you shouldn't dream big, take a big breath and say, as Dolores did: "¡Sí, se puede! Yes, you can!"

ACKNOWLEDGMENTS

....

The author would like to acknowledge the continuing work being done by the Dolores Huerta Foundation (DoloresHuerta.org) in support of community empowerment and social justice.

~ References ~

BOOKS

Bardacke, Frank. *Trampling Out the Vintage: César Chávez and the Two Souls of the United Farm Workers*. Brooklyn, New York: Verso, 2011.

Brill, Marlene Targ. *Dolores Huerta Stands Strong: The Woman Who Demanded Justice*. Athens, Ohio: Ohio University Press, 2018.

Brown, Monica. *Side by Side: The Story of*

Dolores Huerta and César Chávez/Lado a lado: La historia de Dolores Huerta y César Chávez. New York: HarperCollins, 2010.

David, Alexis. *Dolores Huerta, Labor Leader*. Saddleback Educational Publishing, 2022.

García, Mario T., ed. *A Dolores Huerta Reader*. Albuquerque: University of New Mexico Press, 2008.

Griswold del Castillo, Richard, and Richard A. Garcia. *César Chávez: A Triumph of Spirit*. Norman, Okla.: University of Oklahoma Press, 1995. Chapter 4: "Coleadership: The Strength of Dolores Huerta."

Levy, Jacques E., and César Chávez. *César Chávez: Autobiography of La Causa*. Minneapolis: University of Minnesota Press, 2007.

ARTICLES

Bencomo Lobaco, Julia. "Dolores Huerta: The Vision and Voice of Her Life's Work." In García, Mario T., ed. *A Dolores Huerta Reader.* Albuquerque: University of New Mexico Press, 2008. Originally published in AARP *Segunda Juventud,* fall 2004.

Dovere, Edward-Isaac. "This Is a Step Up Above Slavery." *Politico* magazine. September 5, 2017. politico.com/magazine/story/2017/09/05/dolores-huerta-trump-daca-215575/.

Huerta, Dolores. "Dolores Huerta Talks about Republicans, César Chávez, Children, and Her Home Town." In García, Mario T. Ed. *A Dolores Dolores Huerta Reader.* Albuquerque: University of New Mexico Press, 2008. Originally published in *La Voz del Pueblo.* January 25, 1973. 3–4.

Jarrett, Valerie. "Yes, Dolores Can: The 90-Year-Old Activist on Speaking Up, Raising Hell, and Doing the Work." *Glamour*. October 13, 2020. glamour.com/story/dolores-huerta-women-of-the-year-2020.

National Park Service. "Workers United: The Delano Grape Strike and Boycott." nps.gov/articles/000/workers-united-the-delano-grape-strike-and-boycott.htm.

Rose, Margaret. "Dolores Huerta: The United Farm Workers Union." In García, Mario T., ed. *A Dolores Huerta Reader*. University of New Mexico Press, 2008. Originally published in Eric Arnesen, ed., *The Human Tradition in American Labor History*. Wilmington: SR Books, an imprint of Rowman & Littlefield Publishers, Inc. 2004. 211–229.

WEBSITES

doloreshuerta.org/doloreshuerta

doloreshuerta.org/educationpolicy/dolores-huerta
-day-curriculum

dol.gov/general/workcenter/unions-101

glamour.com/story/dolores-huerta-women-of
-the-year-2020

guides.loc.gov/latinx-civil-rights/united-farm
-workers-union

puffinfoundation.org/puffin-prize-for-creative
-citizenship

ufw.org/history-si-se-puede

whitehouse.gov/briefing-room/statements-releases
/2022/07/01/president-biden-announces
-recipients-of-the-presidential-medal-of-freedom

womenshistory.org/education-resources
/biographies/dolores-huerta

VIDEOS

Huerta, Dolores, Peter Bratt, Brian Benson, Carlos Santana, Mark Kilian, and Jessica Congdon. *Dolores*. Educational edition. Sausalito, California: ro*co films educational, 2017.

DR. MONICA BROWN is the award-winning author of many multicultural books for children, including *Frida Kahlo and Her Animalitos*, *Sharuko: El arqueólogo peruano/Peruvian Archaeologist Julio C. Tello*, *Waiting for the Biblioburro/ Esperando el biblioburro*; *Marisol McDonald Doesn't Match/Marisol McDonald no combina*; *Small Room, Big Dreams: The Journey of Julián and Joaquin Castro*; and the Lola Levine chapter book series. Her books have garnered multiple starred reviews and awards, and have appeared in *The New York Times*, *The Washington Post*, and NPR's *All Things Considered*. She teaches at Northern Arizona University and lives in Flagstaff with her family.

Photo credit: Cameron Schmitz

You can visit Monica Brown online at
MonicaBrown.net
or follow her on Twitter
@MonicaBrownBks

GILLIAN FLINT has worked as a professional illustrator since earning an animation and illustration degree in 2003. Her work has since been published in the UK, USA and Australia. In her spare time, Gillian enjoys reading, spending time with her family and pottering about in the garden on sunny days. She lives in the northwest of England.

Courtesy of the illustrator

You can visit Gillian Flint online at
gillianflint.com
or follow her on Instagram
@gillianflint_illustration

CHELSEA CLINTON is the author of the #1 *New York Times* bestseller *She Persisted: 13 American Women Who Changed the World*; *She Persisted Around the World: 13 Women Who Changed History*; *She Persisted in Sports: American Olympians Who Changed the Game*; *She Persisted in Science: Brilliant Women Who Made a Difference*; *Don't Let Them Disappear: 12 Endangered Species Across the Globe*; *Welcome to the Big Kids Club*; *It's Your World: Get Informed, Get Inspired & Get Going!*; *Start Now!: You Can Make a Difference*; with Hillary Clinton, *Grandma's Gardens* and *Gutsy Women*; and, with Devi Sridhar, *Governing Global Health: Who Runs the World and Why?* She is also the Vice Chair of the Clinton Foundation, where she works on many initiatives, including those that help empower the next generation of leaders. She lives in New York City with her husband, Marc, and their children.

Courtesy of the author

You can follow Chelsea Clinton on Twitter
@ChelseaClinton
or on Facebook at
facebook.com/chelseaclinton

ALEXANDRA BOIGER has illustrated nearly twenty picture books, including the She Persisted books by Chelsea Clinton; the popular Tallulah series by Marilyn Singer; and the Max and Marla books, which she also wrote. Originally from Munich, Germany, she now lives outside of San Francisco, California, with her husband, Andrea, daughter, Vanessa, and two cats, Luiso and Winter.

Photo credit: Vanessa Blasich

You can visit Alexandra Boiger online at
alexandraboiger.com
or follow her on Instagram
@alexandra_boiger

Read about more inspiring women in the

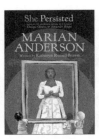   

She Persisted series!

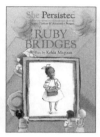

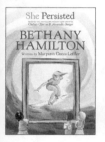
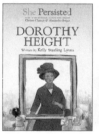

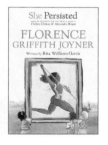

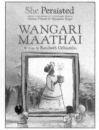

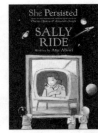
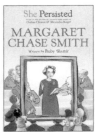

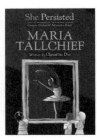

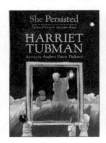
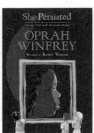